The Spiritual Wisdom of the Syriac *Book of Steps*

Robert A. Kitchen

SLG Press
Convent of the Incarnation Fairacres
Parker Street Oxford OX4 1TB England
www.slgpress.co.uk

First published by SLG Press 2013

ISBN 978-0-7283-0238-9
ISSN 0307-1405

Cover illustration: 'The Ascension' from the Rabbula Gospels, fol. 13v. (Florence, Biblioteca Medicea Laurenziana, cod. Plut. I, 56), a sixth-century illuminated Syriac Gospel book. The Ascension image is referred to by the author of the *Book of Steps (Mēmrā 28).* Used with permission.

Printed by Lightning Source ®
www.lightningsource.com

Typeset by
Oxford eBooks Ltd
www.oxford-ebooks.com

Introduction

The *Book of Steps* has always had trouble getting noticed. The book is a collection of thirty discourses or *mēmrē*, written in the Aramaic dialect of Syriac sometime in the second half of the fourth century. Anonymity is often the sad legacy for ancient texts, but in the case of the *Book of Steps* the author openly intended to remain anonymous. As well, this collection has no real name, the *Book of Steps* being the title suggested by modern scholars. Moreover, the editor of the critical edition, Michael Kmosko, conferred upon the Syriac work the indignity of a Latin name, *Liber Graduum*, and that remains the title by which most scholars and readers recognize the work.

The author of the *Book of Steps* was writing to and about the Christian community in which he lived during the period before monasticism and monasteries had taken their traditional shape. 'Perfection' and 'Uprightness' were life-style choices adopted by committed Christians in the church and community, though these had not become standardized.

The absence of historical and geographical details in the *Book of Steps* stymies attempts to place this book and its author in its natural context. There is one small reference alluding to the Lesser Zab River (in present-day northeast Iraq), and another that seems to suggest the ongoing military and cultural struggle between the Roman and Persian empires. Assuming the community of the *Book of Steps* was situated in the vicinity of the Lesser Zab in the late fourth century, it was clearly within the confines of the Persian Empire, a not-always-benevolent regime that periodically suspected all Christians to be Roman sympathizers at heart. The author refers to incidents of violence inflicted against some of his protégés both from within and without the community. Some of this violence may have had official government sanction.

The style and subject matter of the Book of Steps seem to come from one voice. The diversity of the discourses points to them being the collected works of this anonymous spiritual leader. The author spends considerable time defining the vocation and rules for the Perfect ones (*gmīrē*) and the Upright ones (*kēnē*), the two levels, or steps, of Christian life in their community, since he perceives that the standards for Perfection and Uprightness have regrettably slipped. The last five discourses shift the focus away from the Perfect ones, who have stumbled, towards the Upright who, while living and ministering in the world, have conducted themselves with more integrity and humility. If only they would completely renounce the world and become celibate, the author chides, laments and encourages, the Upright ones would quickly graduate to the level of Perfection.

The Perfect ones of the *Book of Steps* were not perfect, either in theory or in practice. *Gmīrē*, 'the Perfect ones', and *gmīrūtā*, 'Perfection', may be rendered as 'mature ones' and 'maturity', but the latter is not always a satisfactory or fitting label. The author defines the Perfect usually in an apophatic manner relative to the lower level, the Upright ones. That is, the Perfect ones are understood as not doing what the Upright do, but with little precision after that. The Upright pray three times a day, fast twice a week, perform the active ministries of feeding the hungry, clothing the naked, tending to the sick, using their business income to meet the needs of others, and may be married.

The Perfect, on the other hand, pray unceasingly, fast

every day, neither work nor labour, nor perform active ministries to others. Therefore they have no income, no residence, and no wives. Wandering throughout the region, they teach and mediate conflicts. Indeed, a significant part of the eventual backsliding of the Perfect is that they are lured into performing tasks reserved for the Upright ones.

The *Book of Steps* is not a manual of discipline for this pre-monastic community, though the author works hard to develop such a manual in several discourses. Viewing the collection of thirty discourses as a whole, one is able to gain a unique picture of a living Christian community, replete with remarkable ideals, real failures, an impassioned engagement in theological and social controversies, and profound hope for the near future.

Aside from Biblical characters, virtually no personal names are mentioned by the author, yet one can feel tangibly his relationship with a number of people as a spiritual director and pastor. Speaking always in the language of scripture, it is obvious that for him the events and personalities of the Bible are still alive and valid in his day. The fact that the author will amend his strategies and tactics during the course of the Book of Steps demonstrates his primary concern for the individuals under his pastoral care.

Unfortunately, later Syriac literature did not seem to know the *Book of Steps*. There are sixteen manuscripts—more than many other important texts—but only three more or less complete ones. Most of the other manuscripts include merely a discourse or two nestled among larger collections of spiritual writings. Direct citation is found in only two manuscripts (British Library Additional 14193 and Paris Syr. 195, fol. 241b-242a), but the ideas and phrases of the *Book of Steps* do find their way into other works. A surprising location is Saying 27 of the *Gospel of Thomas* that speaks of 'fasting to the world'. Along with the *Book of Steps,* these are the only works where this expression is found.

The principal repository of the thought and institutions of the *Book of Steps* is in the *Ascetical Discourses* of Philoxenus of Mabbug (484-519). Philoxenus, the anti-Chalcedonian bishop of Mabbug in western Syria and colleague of Severus of Antioch, wrote thirteen long sermons about the spiritual life to monks under his pastoral care. He is the only Syriac author to utilize the terminology of the two levels or steps of the Christian life—Perfection and Uprightness—but the social situation had dramatically changed.

A century-and-a-half later, monasticism was in full flower, and Philoxenus deployed the same steps and terminology of Uprightness and Perfection to mark the formal progress of novice and veteran monks. While Philoxenus never cites the *Book of Steps* directly, he appears familiar with its traditions and adapts them to his purpose.

The content of each discourse, or *mēmrā,* below will be summarized in the first paragraph, followed by an indented passage selected to illustrate the author's spiritual perspective and guidance, and then a brief reflection on how this ancient wisdom may be understood today. The references at the end of the citation are the page numbers in The *Book of Steps*: *The Syriac Liber Graduum,* translation & introduction by Robert A. Kitchen & Martien F. G. Parmentier (Cistercian Studies 196; Kalamazoo, Michigan: Cistercian Publications, 2004); the column and line number are of the Syriac text in *Liber Graduum, Patrologia Syriaca 3* edited by M. Kmosko (Paris, 1926).

I hope that this book will enable readers to appreciate and benefit from the practical wisdom on the spiritual life the author offers. For those who remain hungry for more, the full text and commentary noted above remains available to provide a spiritual banquet that keeps filling the table.

Robert A. Kitchen

August 2013

Syriac Editor's Preface

An anonymous Syriac editor introduces the reader to the work of the anonymous author of the *Book of Steps*. While desiring anonymity, the author is acknowledged to be one of the last disciples of the Apostles and one of the first teachers in the Syriac language, although he is a spiritual, not a scholarly, writer. The editor places him in the company of several late fourth-century doctors of the church—Gregory Nazianzus, Basil of Caesarea, Evagrius Ponticus—possibly indicating a mid-to-late fourth-century date for the composition of the original collection. The editor illustrates the author's approach by inserting at the conclusion of this preface the last (and lost) section of the *Book of Steps*.

> You see how the Lord poured out his Spirit at certain times and how sons and daughters prophesy, namely, those who keep the commandments of our Lord and who imitate his humility. See how their tongue is the 'pen of a skilful scribe', that is of our Lord, who is fair and beautiful in countenance (this is something that is beyond comprehension), and their tongue is a pen to him, with which he writes wonderful rules concerning himself, which tell humanity to get to know him and to keep all his commandments. So do not have doubts and say, 'There are no people who prophesy or discourse about God in our time'.
>
> *pp. 5-6; col. 8: lines 9-21; from the 'last section' of the last or thirtieth* mēmrā.

The issue always at hand in spiritual writing and reading is: does this apply to me? Can this still happen now? The author is adamant that the personalities of the Old and New

Testament and the saints of yore are very much alive in the midst of the lives of the Upright and Perfect ones. God still prods people into speaking about divine things, though in a different way and style from that of the Biblical era. It seems that no matter which century, we expect authentically religious people to speak only with a Biblical accent, but there are many who speak and write of the Word with new words.

Mēmrā One
Author's overture

The beginning point is always the Scriptures, but we may discern its contents only when we humble ourselves and submit our minds to the guidance of the Holy Spirit. Those who live in the world necessarily operate by the minor commandments of the Gospel, the rules of the level of uprightness. After Adam fell from Perfection, he remained in the level of uprightness, yet we, having broken the Golden Rule, have fallen below even that state.

> There is a kind of forgiveness that is given to one individual only, such as to the robber who alone was forgiven without having any works to his credit. Other people are not forgiven when they have no works to refer to, only when they have done penance.
>
> If you want to understand why this robber was forgiven: in his case the king came to his door while he was not aware of it. He granted him his petition and forgave him. Our Lord disposes of the things that are his own. To you he says, 'Repent and I will forgive you'. So he showed the richness of his mercy by the example of this one person, in order to encourage the penitent, who keep his commandments in their penance: how great are his mercies that he even had pity on someone who had no works to offer, and yet forgave him!
>
> *p. 12; cols. 21: 23-26, 24: 2-10*

Where the narrative of scripture does not seem to match traditional doctrine and practical theology, the author is willing to adjust and think that God is right and exceptions become the rule. The thief on the cross next to Jesus possesses no obvious virtues and exhibits no particular penance, yet the mercy and grace of God become the rule. As much as we try to codify God's rules, the author knows that our understanding of God's economy can be skewed by our own self-interests. Some might presume to call this perspective 'post-modern'. It just might mean that early Christian writers were more perceptive of the human spirit than we give them credit. The rule is, watch what God does and is doing, which can make for an exceptional love and life.

Mēmrā Two
About those who want to become perfect

Perfection is attained through fulfilling the major commandments, by which one becomes humble and sees the Lord in the Spirit during this life. Those who keep the major commandments eat from the trees of the spiritual paradise, while the minor commandments are like milk and honey for those pursuing the lesser path. One tactic of the Evil One is to trick one into not going beyond the minor commandments, yet through the Paraclete—the full and complete gift of the Holy Spirit—one can surpass and live beyond even the major commandments.

> If one is prepared to try, it will prove possible not only to surpass the minor commandments for the sake of love, but even the major ones. Our Lord said: To him who strikes you on the cheek, offer the other; also. Let such a person yield his back too, and then he will be greater than him who only presents his cheek. Let such

a one never seek any revenge at all, and then he will be greater than him who only forgives seventy times seven. Let him go more than [just] a [few] mile[s], and then he will have humbled himself more than Jesus commanded. For he said: If anyone presses you for to go one mile, go two more with him.

In so treating the minor commandments, he will become ready for the major ones. Then he will teach the adulterers in peace, and be greater than him who does not eat bread with them, who does not mix with them at all. So he teaches his brother in private not to sin. Such a person will also be greater than those who condemn and dishonour him. Thus he will outgrow the minor commandments, stand fast in the major ones and become Perfect.

And he who stands fast in the major commandments, which are gentle, will [go on to] lower himself more than is prescribed by the major commandments. Then he is glorified with our Lord and has become greater than others who are standing fast in them. For it is possible to become greater than other people through the Spirit, the Paraclete, when one lowers oneself more than is required by the commandments. Likewise, our Lord said: If I, then, your Lord and Teacher, who have not sinned or erred, have lowered myself so much, how much more ought not you, who are servants and sinners, to lower yourselves. For since I have lowered myself before evildoers, how much more ought not you to lower yourself before evil people!

pp. 20-21; cols. 41: 3 – 44: 13

One can never be good enough, and certainly never perfect enough. The author knows that being satisfied with one's moral status is a mortal wound. There is no final achievement of perfection in which one can rest and reap the benefits. That's why the term 'perfection' is somewhat misleading: perfection normally implies completeness, but the author urges us always onward. Once one has attained the canonical qualifications of Christian perfection, don't think you are allowed to stop. Don't think you have done it all upon mastering the major commandments of the Gospel, or that you can do it all by your own will and energy. The Spirit will take you where you cannot go by yourself. So, you can never be too humble.

Mēmrā Three
The physical and the spiritual ministry

The Upright ones will receive a lesser portion of the kingdom than the Perfect, engaging in a ministry to the physical needs of others while not giving up either their own possessions or their marriages. The Perfect ones perform the spiritual ministries of prayer, counselling and teaching, while not being involved in commerce and worldly problems. Originally, God desired that no one would have to work, but Adam's sin prevented that divine strategy from being realized. Work is good, but nevertheless is a consequence of a human desire to become God.

> For Spirit-filled people treat all people with discernment. They show him who makes the effort to reach Perfection how to get there; and they make him into a spiritual minister in the ministry wherein the Spirit

> and salvation are found. They make the person who does not strive and seek this portion into a minister of physical things, that is, of what is visible, performing a visible service. Whoever is in the Spirit, however, ministers to what is invisible for corporeal eyes, namely to the soul, which is visible in the Spirit for the spiritual eye. Really, it is an easy enterprise for everybody; the only thing necessary is a deliberate effort of the will to empty and lower oneself, and then one can reach the highest level of Perfection. Then one will lower oneself even more and share in the glory of our Lord.
>
> *p. 37; col. 81: 11-25*

The best kind of people—those filled to the brim with the Holy Spirit—neither judge nor condemn nor evaluate other people, but find the best way to use their talents and spirits. The Perfect ones are meant to be doctors of the soul, spirits in a material world, in which she who would be great must humble and lower herself more and more. Those who retain no worldly prestige are the ones who sit next to our Lord.

It really isn't that easy. What early Greek-speaking Christians called *kenosis*—the self-emptying of God and of human beings—flows against the normal patterns of human behaviour and self-image. Grace alone carries a human being in the perfect direction.

Mēmrā Four
On the vegetables for the sick

The diet of 'vegetables for the sick' is detailed, a regimen designed for those still weak in the faith and susceptible to temptations. Procedures and controls are outlined for those who feel compelled to admonish others. Better yet, the author emphasizes, do not judge lest you be judged. Transform the hostile words of enemies into harmless ones and you will frustrate the Evil Ones by your gentleness to the good and bad alike.

> When you meet people who are at enmity with each other, say, 'Brothers, blessed are the peacemakers, for they shall be called sons of God'. Now peacemakers are those who reconcile enemies who belong to other churches, away from their own. They make peace in the land of their Father, and are mediators who reconcile people by imploring them, demonstrating lowliness to them, and admonishing them. When they try to reconcile enemies who speak ill of each other because of their mutual hate, we must transform this speech and instead speak good of them in this way: 'What if I tell you that the person you hate is very sorry he is not on good terms with you, and he wants to make it up with you?' He says, 'I am unhappy about this animosity; Satan has tempted me to abuse my brother, who is a member of me'. Even if he, whoever he is, has not said it this way, it will create a pause until the anger of those who are so far apart has cooled down, and they come to greet each other with a holy kiss. If we do not transform their harmful words into

> harmless ones, as a result of all the spiteful remarks they make about each other, what a fine mediator you will make if you go and retell each side's exact words to the other! You will just stir up more trouble and they will not even be reconciled.
>
> *pp. 43-44; cols. 93: 22 – 96: 18*

No one who ventures out on a spiritual journey can avoid peace. Yet among human beings, peace seldom is born, but must be made. A primary calling of the Perfect ones is to reconcile those who are in conflict with one another. Talking separately with the antagonists about how their enemy regrets the enmity he or she has helped create, the Perfect ones transform harmful words into harmless words to help create a breathing space for empathy. Perhaps this seems naive, but the genius of such simplicity is its gracefulness. The next breath is a holy kiss.

Mēmrā Five
On the milk of the children

The 'diet of milk' consists of rules intended for the spiritually immature ones in the community who should avoid associating with sinners for the time being. Gradually, one may come to mix with sinners without imitating, exposing or condemning them. Jesus educated disciples to lead others to Perfection, as Simon Peter did with respect to unclean food. The Paraclete, the fullness of the Holy Spirit, however, comes only to those who are strangers to the world. The reception of the Paraclete is the beginning of the way to complete Perfection, for one keeps growing until death.

> For how do you know, you who are angry with a wrongdoer, if he is not another Paul, or one of the publicans, a Zacchaeus or a Matthew, or a Rahab the harlot, or someone like that Samaritan woman who committed adultery with many men, about whom our Lord testified that she had had five husbands besides the one she had at the time he met her? All these people repented and were saved. Should we then exalt ourselves above sinners, without knowing ourselves whether we will end up as a Solomon or as Iscariot, or like the others who were good to begin with but sinned in the end?
>
> *p. 47; col. 104: 13-24*

Humility is unrelenting. The author insists that one should allow and acknowledge that the grace of God may capture anyone. God has chosen some surprising people, people clearly morally inferior to you and me. Where does that leave righteous you and me? 'Consider everyone else better than yourself' (Phil. 2: 3) is the antiphonal refrain of the author, and then you will be blessed with the opportunity to serve every person. Perhaps then you may be chosen for something surprising.

Mēmrā Six
On those who are made perfect and continue to grow

The author utilizes metaphors of the crafting of royal jewel chests and gold vessels to parallel the preparation of a person for Perfection. Once the Perfect one has received the full share of the Holy Spirit, the Paraclete, he is able to defeat

Satan, dwell in the spiritual Eden, and grow to the level of the angels.

> So it is also with a person once he has lowered himself from all things that are on earth, has subdued his mind night and day, who counts everyone else better than himself, has emptied himself of all he possessed, and kisses the feet of his enemies. Our Lord will look upon this person's lowliness and send him the Spirit, the Paraclete, and he shall know the whole truth.
>
> *p. 62; col. 141: 7-14*

For the author of the *Book of Steps* this is the way the Gospel dresses itself, with the clothes of lowliness and humility by which one understands the whole truth. The literal sense of the phrase 'subdue one's mind' is to 'break one's mind'—a harsher verb, but the ascetical life has its harsh junctures at which gentler measures often open doors for the Antagonist. Many contemplative religious traditions prefer 'breaking the mind' as the idiom for making the human mind realize it is not as big as God.

Mēmrā Seven
On the commandments of the Upright

This is a discourse on the way of Uprightness for those who have chosen not to take the hard road of Perfection. One begins by following the Ten Commandments and the Golden Rule. The Upright ones must avoid dealing with any kind of magic or magicians, for a person dies or lives according to God's decision, not Satan's. The Upright ones are given a medical ministry to those who need to be physically healed.

> Moreover, just as he does not want a person to curse him, not even when he makes a mistake, if he turns away from hating the one who shows him up, he would like them to forgive him when he is caught in transgression whether in adultery or in stealing. Even if he should go as far as to kill someone, he wants people to forgive him when he asks this from them. He should act similarly to whomever injures him with wrongs such as these, and [thereby] become an Upright one. Just as he would like someone to feed him when hungry and to refresh him when thirsty, and when he travels in a foreign country [to have someone] bring him into a shelter in winter and into the shade in the summer and give him what he needs, and just as he would like someone to clothe him when naked and give him shoes when barefoot, so he should do to others, his fellow human beings.
>
> *p. 66; col. 148: 7-22*

Here is the Golden Rule read honestly. The moral worthiness of one's fellow human being ('son of one's flesh', literally) is not what matters. Put yourself in his or her place and feel their distress, even if they have brought it upon themselves. 'A wretch like me' would desperately want kindness and physical aid in the most ignominious moments, so nothing less is required of you when someone else is in need. After all, as the author noted in *Mēmrā* Four above, 'my brother or sister is a member of me'.

Mēmrā Eight
On one who gives all he has to feed the poor

This is another discourse directed to the Upright ones, particularly to those who in ministering to the poor and hungry give away all they possess. While the Upright one is perceived as nothing by a Perfect one if he does not empty himself and renounce the world, the author affirms that, nevertheless, the Upright one will receive the reward of salvation, albeit a lesser portion.

> For he who gives all he has to feed the poor on account of God and renounces—as [the Lord] said to him—all he possesses, but does not have in him that humble love that loves his murderers and washes the feet of his enemies and considers everyone better than himself, giving heed to heaven and not to earth, his mind serving there in the heavenly Jerusalem, bound there to our Lord, [then, without this, he is nothing].
>
> *p. 82; col. 193: 1-9*

Going through the motions of the Biblical commandments—feeding the hungry, clothing the naked—is not the whole Gospel. It is not really in the doing of the commandments but in becoming the person who does the commandments that one progresses towards perfection. Time and again, the anonymous author insists that one is something only in loving and serving the worst people, and in knowing that one is no better than they are.

Mēmrā Nine
On Uprightness and the love of the Upright and of the Prophets

The author offers an extended Biblical exposition to explain how the Old Testament prophets were ordered by God on certain occasions to act violently against his enemies—reducing their personal status below the level of Uprightness. The prophets eventually are admitted into the kingdom following the admittance of the Apostles. The author demonstrates that God sets the agenda with the long view in mind, even while God's way does not match our rational understanding.

Next, let us talk about the love of our fathers because we should imitate their love and their lowliness. Abraham and Isaac pursued Perfection when their wives were taken from them and they did not quarrel or fight. When the well was taken from them, they neither quarrelled nor became their enemies. They endured the rape of their riches with joy, and were held captive neither by their possession nor by their wives, as [they were] by the love of and desire for God.

If the Lord had said to them, 'Renounce your wives and let go of your property,' as he had said to the apostles, they would have done his will, just as when he had said to them, 'Go out from your land and from your family, and go where I tell you'. Because they loved him and loved [fellow] human beings, they went gladly, even while they knew that they had been plundered and cheated and had their wives taken, in order that they might fulfil the commandment of him whom they loved, and in order to continue honouring those whom they loved. Also, whenever he asked them to sacrifice their sons, they gladly sacrificed, because his love was fixed in their heart and they did his will in all he commanded them.

But had [God] said to them, 'Give up your wives and your sons and your possessions, and go proclaim me wherever I will tell you', it would have been easier for them to leave their wives in celibacy and their living children in their homes and their wealth and everything that belonged to them with their families and go wherever the Lord sent them; much more easily than what he did say to them, 'Go with everything you have with you', because their women were carried away by force to be dishonoured before their very eyes, and their sons to be sacrificed in the face of [their sense] of compassion, and their possessions were to be plundered every day as they looked on with their own eyes and endured it—because of the hope of truth, which is to come. But all whom the Lord held back from renunciation and from physical celibacy were to become an example to all who are married in this world, so that they might live like them.

pp. 101-2; cols. 241: 4 – 244: 22

The preferred way of Perfection necessarily involves the renunciation of property and desire for this world, as well as celibacy. Yet, the author realizes that everything does not work perfectly, and that God often seems to choose the less than ideal as the vehicle by which people see and experience the reality of the kingdom. Abraham and Isaac could have been good celibate ascetics in the Christian mould, but God told them instead to 'go with everything you have'. The Upright ones, married, worldly and wealthy, have no less an important assignment to live God's way fully. God sorts it all out in the end, though few of us can ever figure out the maths.

Mēmrā Ten

The author delivers a sermon arguing against a spiritualizing asceticism that has arisen among the community in which physical fasting is disdained by those who believe they are so spiritually advanced that they have superseded any physical discipline.

> Gluttony harms bodies [even] when they are healthy, and hateful words and everything evil harm the soul. In other words, if the soul is harmed, the body is harmed; and if the body is harmed, the soul is harmed. For there is no inner person without an outer [person], and there is no outer [person] without an inner. But if you wish to become perfect and be made pure, pursue justice of the heart and of the body and [pursue] sincerity, lowliness, and peace of the heart and body. Because soul and body mutually succeed and fail with one another, together they are praised and together they sit down at table, and those who keep his commandments with their bodies and souls will rest together on the day of the Lord.
>
> *p. 107; cols. 253: 19 – 256: 5*

In a sermon addressed to his congregation the author makes clear that Christian asceticism is not a battle of soul against body, but that the human being is a unified whole. The extremes of asceticism do not find a place in the community of the *Book of Steps*, nor does a libertarian attitude that disdains doing anything physical because one is now spiritually superior. Syriac Christianity would become infamous for its emphasis upon a severe physical asceticism that perceived the body and its desires as a hindrance to the quest for holiness. This particular community is striking, almost singular, because apparently it does not advocate such extremes. While fasting, celibacy, and homelessness are the physical demands on the Perfect, and to a lesser degree on the Upright, the Christian will discover sanctity only within this material and bodily world.

Mēmrā Eleven

Although one must be able to distinguish between the major and minor commandments of Scripture, the author defends his position that Scripture is intended for and may be interpreted by two or more levels of Christians among its readers.

> Which of these commandments does the one who says they are spoken to a single person choose: the major one or the minor one? [Would you choose] that major one which [says] 'Make your soul lowly', and 'Consider your brother better than yourself', or that minor one, 'Do not eat with immoral people'? If you keep that major one, you shall receive a blessing from God. If you choose that minor one, the greater part of the world will become impure in your eyes. Satan even will make the pure ones [appear] defiled in your

> eyes because you permit him to have power over you. Therefore, if you keep that major commandment, you will ascend from the minor one. If you choose that minor one, you will fall short of that major one.
>
> *p. 116; col. 280: 2-15*

The major and minor commandments of Scripture, which are addressed generally to the Perfect and the Upright respectively, follow the lines of the struggle between two ways of relating to people. The perfect way is not to be worried about anyone; while the upright way is always cautious about being wrongly influenced. Once you start worrying, the author confides, you will worry about everyone—and it is difficult to be Christian by yourself.

The Bible, moreover, is not to be shackled to one interpretative scheme only. The author knew that to limit the meaning of any particular Biblical narrative to a single solution would spell the death of Scripture's spirit and power. It is a Scripture far more complex than one person can systematically determine, and it still reads that way today, except for those who are determined to read it only their way and pronounce anyone else wrong.

Mēmrā Twelve
On the hidden and public ministry of the Church

The Church exists on three levels: the Visible Church, the Church of the Heart, and the Hidden Church. The true church is the Visible, physical, and earthly church through which one must travel to the Church of the Heart and the Hidden heavenly Church.

> For our Lord and his first and last preachers did not erect in vain the Church and altar and baptism, all of which are visible to physical eyes. It is through these visible things, however, that we shall be in these heavenly things, which are invisible to eyes of the flesh, our bodies becoming temples and our hearts altars. Let us open [the door] and enter into this visible church with its priesthood and its worship so that [our bodies] may become good examples to all people who imitate [the church] in the vigils and fasting and patience of our Lord and his preachers—let us act and teach.
>
> But if we doubt and treat with contempt this public church and this public altar and the public priesthood and the baptism that brings forgiveness, our body will not become a temple, nor will our heart become an altar and a fortress of glory. That higher church and its altar, its light and its priesthood, will not be revealed to us. Whither are gathered all the saints who are pure in their heart and dwell in its glory and luxuriate in its light for they do not treat with contempt this blessed nurse who gives birth everyday and educates good envoys and sends [them] to that great church in heaven.
>
> *pp. 120-1; cols. 288: 20 – 289:5 & 289:14 – 292:1*

While the author aspires to the higher and heavenly church, he does not countenance any denigration of what goes on in the visible earthly church. It is not just that the visible church is the model of that higher state; it remains the only place in which we truly live as the church. The author sounds the same alarm as in *Mēmrā* Ten, that the spiritual life never leaves behind the physical life. Granted, life in this earthly church can still be frustrating and maddening, and while it is fashionable in some circles to declare that one can be a Christian without the Church—and therefore without all the troublesome people—Christianity is at heart the way to live with other human beings and the other parts of God's creation.

Mēmrā Thirteen
By the same author on the ways of the Upright

This discourse presents the most detailed description of the Upright ones. The focus is upon the Upright one's social obligations and ministry to others, particularly marriage, commerce, and providing for the needy.

> Uprightness's love does not withhold any possession it has, whether of food or drink or clothing; but it will give liberally to everyone, to the good and the bad. Once evening is come [Uprightness] reconciles with whoever is angry with her, [and] if [the angry person] is persuaded, [well and good]. If not, however, she commits the judgment to our Lord. Between her and her neighbour she seeks [only] what is owed her, and does not put him to shame before the community. If someone steals from her and she catches him, she takes back what is hers and releases him without dishonour. If he has nothing, she releases him without disgrace and does not despise the person who sins against her.
>
> *p. 130; col. 313: 3-14*

The step of Uprightness is personified in the feminine throughout the *mēmrā*, since Uprightness is a feminine noun. While it is not a move towards inclusive language or feminist imagery, the author provides a perspective that should not be overlooked. The Upright ones are more than ordinary Christians who covenant to carry out the heavy physical labour of Christian charity. Whether it is giving away something to the needy, reconciling conflicts and property disputes, the Upright one—any Christian—operates by grace that perceives a human being in trouble, not someone who has wronged you. Perfection is only a breath away from such an ordinary Christian who deals with people in this manner. The author is caught in the tension between the spiritual elitism he promotes in the Church, and the spiritual reality that God does not distinguish between people except by how they love one another.

Mēmrā Fourteen
On the Upright and the Perfect

The author presents a series of dichotomies describing first the Upright ones in terms of their duties, avoidance of evil actions, and their emotions and attitudes. Juxtaposed to the Upright are the Perfect ones, who always transcend these worldly parameters and conflicts, Christians who find no limits in their godly behaviour.

> The Upright are sanctified from the evil of the earth, [but] not from its possessions, its benefits, or its fellowship; but the Perfect rise above every inheritance of the visible earth and above all its evils and its possession and riches, and above temporal

intercourse and all its delights.

The Upright build and possess, not as [if] forever, but live in the world as strangers; the Perfect neither build nor possess, nor do their minds abide on the earth.

pp. 135-6; cols. 324: 11 – 325: 6, 10-13

The author contrasts—in an almost adversarial fashion—the practical spirituality of both the Upright and Perfect. Maybe all people are created equal, but inequalities do develop, so there are different paths and different rewards. Inferior though their path may be to the Perfect, the Upright ones are nonetheless summoned to a rarefied calling, for they live in the world as strangers. Being a stranger is an awful feeling, yet incredibly freeing, for the world no longer has a hold over you. The Perfect ones obviously live in the world as well, but strive to remain completely aloof from the business and pleasure of the world. In most churches we work to be friends to strangers so that they are no longer strangers. Paradoxically, the Gospel life is always nudging and shoving us to be both friend and stranger in a foreign land, to live in, but not be of, the world.

Mēmrā Fifteen
On Adam's marital desire

The author gives a long discourse on the origins and consequences of the human sexual drive. Celibacy, a principal requirement for Perfection, is considered the proper channel for sexuality. Sexual lust is not innate in human beings, but derives from the temptations of Satan. Consequently, marriage is provisionally sanctioned by a merciful, albeit disappointed, God.

Therefore, those who do good and are honest some of the time, but sometimes treat a person poorly, do not abide either with Uprightness or with evil, being familiar with both. As with today, we see people who do what is below the Upright, these who are inferior to the Perfect. The Upright are those who utilize the good things, while not treating anyone badly. Those who do good half [of the time] and [do] evil [the other] half, even if they are chastened, God is merciful to them because they have been merciful to people. Those whose good deeds are fewer than their evil deeds, God is not unjust in forgetting their [good] deeds; just as he will repay them for their evil deeds, so also [God will repay them for] their good deeds.

Those who were without good deeds and without evil actions, and who neither treated anyone well nor badly, will not descend to Gehenna nor will inherit the Kingdom. They are considered better than Gehenna and live in the place that suits them, and our Lord does to them whatever he wishes. While they have not treated anyone badly, still they have withheld from everyone their compassion. They have kept that word, 'Whoever does evil will be tormented', but have abandoned that [other] word, 'Whoever does good will inherit eternal life'. Therefore, they deprived their souls of pleasure and guarded their souls from torment.

pp. 147-8; cols. 357: 18 – 360: 16

It is apparent that the author does not live in an isolated community. Certainly, he would prefer all people to become perfect, but he recognizes that the grey areas of spirituality flourish more than the extremes of Perfection and shameless profligacy. Most of us do sin a little and do some good. The author encourages such people to keep up the fight for good against evil, that all is not lost, and that there is a reward awaiting you, albeit smaller if you are not 'Perfect'. The author does not spell it out, but the fate of the person who seemingly stays aloof from human affairs and does nothing is eternal boredom.

Mēmrā Sixteen
On how a person may surpass the major commandments

The author insists that one can continue to grow above and beyond the step of Perfection by superseding any quantifiable definitions of Perfection. The model of the holy fool is presented as an ideal of the Perfect life which knows no limits.

> Let me describe for you a foolish person, so that when you see a fool who treats himself with contempt and does not own a house or a wife and any property, not even [extra] garments besides his clothes, nor food apart from a day-to-day [supply], say, 'These are my [ways of life] and I should imitate them'. When you see him talking insanely with everyone—and [if] he establishes a law for himself so that he may not become angry in order not to be found at fault, and [if] he despises the wisdom [of] the wise sage of the world and the philosopher because he is contemptuous of whatever is visible—say, 'These are mine, this is the

> madness of the apostles'.
>
> The fools of the world, in their foolishness, are not able to distinguish between whoever is dishonouring them and whoever is honouring them, and they would be talking first thing in the morning with that one who struck them in the evening. Imitate them in this way. Enter [the home of] the people who are insolent to you as a fool and talk with them and honour those who honour you. Look at the fool who cannot distinguish good people from bad in his foolishness, and in the same way you should love the good and the bad while knowing them [for who they are].
>
> *pp. 164-5; col. 401: 18 – 404: 4 & 7-17*

Simply stated, if you want to be Perfect, be a fool for Christ. Whereas later fools would challenge the powers-that-be with an audacity no others could muster, the author has a specific appreciation of what foolishness is. The fool retains no concept or awareness of the goodness or malevolence of people, or of his or her own honour or shame. A human being is worth treating well, no matter how that person treats the fool. Even the church counsels you against being subjected to such indignities, but the perfect fool does not care. Perfection really has no limits or limitations.

Mēmrā Seventeen
On the sufferings of our Lord who became through them an example for us

This is a discourse on the distinction between sufferings and signs. The imitation of the sufferings of Jesus is the way for those who believe that Jesus is God, while signs are used for those who do not believe in God. The prime example of Jesus' suffering is the occasion when he washed the feet of Iscariot before he washed those of Simon Peter.

> Look, is it not evident that our Lord suffers secretly with us? He was tempted, but he did not abolish our temptations. He suffers with those who suffer and are tempted. See how he suffers secretly, as our Lord said, 'Whoever dishonours you, dishonours me; and whoever honours you, honours me'. Certainly, [our Lord] had suffered well before Paul spoke about it, so then this could only mean that our Lord will come again, suffering physically. But if we give ourselves over to sufferings, our Lord is there to suffer secretly with us.
>
> Therefore, when you read that our Lord purified the lepers and opened [the eyes of] the blind, made the crooked straight, strengthened the paralyzed, calmed the people with dropsy, healed the sick, caused the lame to leap as harts, and straightened the tongues of the dumb, these are signs that our Lord did for whoever does not believe so that they may believe. But signs are not necessary for whoever does believe; yet suffering is necessary for him so that he may be perfected and suffer and mature and be glorified.
>
> *p. 170; cols. 416: 21 – 417: 17*

This is the gospel of asceticism, that through suffering ('the passions') Christ becomes part of you and you become part of Christ. Becoming perfect is not rising above suffering, but becoming one with Christ who suffers secretly with us in our temptations. The most difficult suffering is not physically painful, but overcoming the spiritual pain of a failed relationship, as in the case of Jesus washing the feet of his betrayer Judas before washing those of his faithful disciple Simon.

Mēmrā Eighteen
On the tears of prayer

A meditation on the necessity of agony and struggle in prayer, that is, the mournful tears of prayer which eliminate sin from within and enable one to be perfected.

> Our Lord taught us these things, so that when we are without external sins we should approach the struggle of prayer, as our Lord said and did. Paul said to the brothers who are [living] in our Lord, 'Epaphras does battle for you with his prayer'. This means, our Lord groaned mightily and was afflicted in prayer; his sweat became as clots of blood and he shed many tears so that he might show us that when we are without external sins and open faults, we should offer petition and prayer.
>
> But until we are afflicted in prayer like him and shed tears as he shed and powerfully implore as he implored, we will not be rescued from the sin that dwells in the heart, or from the evil thoughts that we inwardly think. So it is fitting for the men who are in Christ to raise their hands in every region and in every place without anger and without evil thoughts, having shed tears in their love for our Lord and in their yearning for him. At that time let us go and see him face to face, as it is written, 'Blessed are those who are pure in their heart for they shall see God'. In this

> world, as Paul said, we see our Lord with the eyes of our hearts as in a mirror; but in that [other] world, [we will see him] face to face.
>
> *pp. 179-80; cols. 437: 7 – 440: 9*

The Eastern tradition of tears wells up in the prayer of the author. These are not tears caused or brought on by pain or personal problems, but tears viscerally wept in imitation of Christ. Prayer is not merely petition, but a physical form of asceticism aimed at accompanying Jesus in his sufferings and afflictions. Slouching towards Perfection, one starts to see the face of God more clearly through the tears.

Mēmrā Nineteen
On the discernment of the way of perfection

The longest *mēmrā* presents the metaphor of a steep, narrow, and difficult road climbing to the heavenly city of the Perfect. Twenty-five pairs of Biblical citations distinguish between the steep road of the Perfect and the paths diverting to the side of the road intended for the 'sick' and 'children' until they gain enough strength to resume travel on the road.

> This is the perfect road: 'Blessed are those who are pure in their heart, for they shall see God'. But the path which leads you away from it is this: 'If he does not say to you, "I repent", do not forgive him'.
>
> This is written to whomever is stiff-necked and corrupt so that he may be humbled and avoid the evil road and say, 'I will not act like this', and then he shall be forgiven and become a warning and a chastisement to others not to become presumptuous and slack.

> This is [the task] of the leaders and not of the Perfect. The Perfect do not come near the positions of leadership, but if they are [in] leadership positions and are pursuing Perfection, they should leave these positions. Then they can be perfected because the Perfect teach everyone with lowliness and are not able to coerce a person like the rulers [do]. But the leaders, who have authority over each place, are allowed to demand everything justly and to chastise appropriately whoever rebels against [his] companions and exile him until he repents. And because of this it is said, 'Speak and exact [punishment]'.
>
> Those who exact judgment and raise charges are not able to be perfected and become peaceful and kind ones. But if they wish to become upright and pursue Uprightness through these minor commandments and be virtuous on that day of our Lord, but are not able to do the Perfect will of our Lord, as long as they are managing the congregations, they are not able to leave these minor commandments and come to the major commandments. It is in these [major commandments] that the perfect and acceptable will of our Lord resides, and [through them] they will eat solid food and be perfected through suffering, lowliness, and spiritual service.
>
> *pp. 198-9; cols. 492: 23 – 496: 9*

Is there any hope for the government? The author is adamant that being involved in government disqualifies one from the pursuit of Perfection, for proper government requires coercion and violence. Imbued with a strong sense of humility that admits one may not always be right and just, the Perfect ones teach all kinds of people. Coercion, however, is an act of self-assured righteousness that is the antithesis of true humility and lowliness. Here and in other places, the author allows that, yes, someone has to keep the conflicting segments of society in order and discipline, but at a spiritual price. Governmental leaders can, nevertheless, maintain Uprightness if they consciously adhere to the minor commandments. No governmental leader can become a true saint, and no saint can become a governmental leader. But is this government that the author perceives capable of any higher functions, such as maintaining social justice for all?

Mēmrā Twenty
On the difficult steps that are on the road of the city of our Lord

Continuing the same metaphor of the steep road to the heavenly city of the Perfect, the pilgrimage intensifies with the three most difficult steps. Reconciliation with one's enemies and renouncing work in order to divest oneself of every possession are the first two. The last step is the uprooting of the root of sin that Adam had experienced in Eden. One must be prepared to adopt the affliction of prayer in mounting the last step, as witnessed by Jesus before his disciples in Gethsemane.

> So you see, my son, how our Lord became an example for us. See how he went back and forth praying and rousing his disciples so that they might see how he triumphed and [how] they might win like him. For if he himself had had need of prayer, he would have

prayed by himself, and he would have been heard as he was in fact heard. But so that he might make everyone know that he himself had no need of prayer, he went back and forth to his disciples and roused them to teach them how they should pray like him, as he had taught them fasting and battle in his forty days' fast and in his battle with Satan, being tempted by [Satan] as if he were a human being. Our Lord was patient in order to be an example for us to imitate.

Moreover, see how much our Lord prolonged his prayer; in this way he wrestled mightily in his prayer so that from evening until that time when the cock crowed, when the crucifiers seized him, 'he prayed intensely and went back and forth three times to his disciples and said to them, "Stay awake and pray lest you enter into temptation".' See how I pray and I win; you should pray like this and defeat death and sin.

Sin fought during that night with the disciples, and lulled them with the burden of sleep and anxiety, in that [our Lord] had said to them, 'Today I will be delivered up'. In this way [sin] burdened them and did not allow them to see how our Lord wrestled in his prayer. Our Lord had it written down about the struggle he had made with death and placed it in the New Testament so we might act like him and conquer as he had conquered. But, nevertheless, every day our Lord had wrestled in this way with powerful groaning and tears, with great supplication and many prostrations.

p. 218; cols. 548: 17 – 552: 4

The author of the *Book of Steps* does not delve into the mysteries of Christological controversy—it was a little too early for such concerns anyway. Nevertheless, he does slip into his musings an understanding of the nature of Christ and his purpose. Rather than emphasizing atonement, Jesus's mission is presented as an example for human beings in how to live perfectly and spiritually. There is no doubt that for the author Jesus is Lord and God, and therefore not subject to the usual human limitations. So when Jesus attempts to demonstrate and elicit effective prayer to and out of the disciples in Gethsemane, his back-and-forth entreaties to stay awake are the result of his desire to teach them something he has no need to do. The perfect spiritual life is difficult, for it is not an idea, but an incarnation. We lose sight of this life not when we forget its ways, but when we sleep through it. The author's portrayal of Jesus as an example is a little clumsy, yet it is in Jesus's life that one sees most clearly perfection as a human possibility.

Mēmrā Twenty-One
On the tree of Adam

Jesus, now called metaphorically the Tree of Life, is the fulfilment of what Adam was meant to become in the Garden before he sinned. Perfection recaptures and relives the status Adam and Eve possessed and enjoyed before the Fall.

> Adam and Eve desired all these things but were humbled through the mediation of the Evil One and they abandoned heaven and the heavenly wealth and loved the earth and all that is in it. However, Adam and Eve were naked without this visible clothing in

> this world. Adam and Eve had been like this before they had sinned, and it was not that they did not know they had sinned by their rebellion. In this they, however, were foolish for they had hoped to become like God. They erred because there is nothing that is able to become like the Creator of all the worlds, that one who is the Creator, and who is our Lord Jesus Christ. But God saw and averted [his eyes] and was patient and forbearing while Adam despised his words and broke his commandments and sought to usurp, to become the equal of God in majesty, but not in lowliness.
>
> *p. 242; cols. 613: 20 – 616: 10*

> For nothing brought down Adam on the day he fell, except the pride by which he desired to become the equal of God in his majesty. Too much [pride] forced him to depart from the Paradise of the Kingdom and humbled him down to earth.
>
> *p. 243; cols. 616: 24 – 617: 3*

The Story for the early Syriac church was not the Exodus or the Sinai Covenant, but the events of the Garden of Eden. Even the Gospel narratives about Jesus simply complete or restore the original story in Eden. In common with other Syriac writers, the author does not understand the tragedy of Eden to be based in sexuality, but in Adam and Eve lusting—and most of us still lust—to become and act like God. A foolish, impossible thought for any human being, for what creature can alter and reverse the nature of things and become the creator? This is nothing but the end result of a non-humility, whose pride seeks the equality of God in majesty, but not equality in lowliness and humility. The most difficult task is to accept and act simply as who we are as human beings—for which there is more grace than we can imagine.

Mēmrā Twenty-Two
On the judgments that do not save those who observe them

Apparently in this community, Uprightness is often dismissed as merely the application of 'an eye for an eye', but the author emphasizes that this level has advanced well beyond the ethos of the *lex talionis*. For some situations, God has appointed evil judges and kings to judge people harshly, yet restrains their evil tendencies. For the Upright, therefore, the Ten Commandments and the Gospel are sufficient for salvation.

> In this way again let us imitate him, when he calls and has pity upon the tax-collectors and the prostitutes, while submitting himself before one who is inferior to him and is baptized—although [he did] not need [to be]—to be an example for us, so that we might be blessed by one who is less than us and needy of us. Let us imitate him, when he greets his servants and women-servants, preceding them in greeting, and when he impoverished himself and had nowhere to place his head upon the earth, so that we might become rich in his poverty; and when he makes himself a sinner and prays and makes supplication as an offender and makes himself Sin on account of our iniquity so that we might become righteousness through him.
>
> *p. 261; col. 661: 2-14*

The personal example Jesus unveils before us is one of ascetic self-denial and identity with the poor and less virtuous. Jesus is socially radical, initiating the customary greeting to slaves and women, and in this way tendering them honour in the first place and placing himself below their social status. This self-deprecation is not meant just to be admired, but imitated. We can become rich through his poverty and righteous through his assumption of sin-fullness.

Mēmrā Twenty-Three
On Satan and Pharaoh and the Israelites

The author develops an extended Biblical exposition on how God permits free will in evil people, in this case Pharaoh. God did not predestine the hardness of heart of Pharaoh, for such stubbornness was derived from Satan. God's kindness, though, elicited the rebellion of Pharaoh, just as Jesus' humility brought out resistance among the Jewish leaders.

> He also had said regarding Pharaoh, 'I have established him for a controversy', in that when [the Lord] sent punishment upon him, he said to Moses, 'Pray that [this plague] may pass and I will obey and allow you and your people to go in peace.' This is how the Lord hardened him: in that [God] had heard everything [Pharaoh] had called upon him through Moses, and he had healed the land from wounds; thus the listening ear and tolerance of the Lord hardened Pharaoh. For when the suffering arrived, [Pharaoh] was humbled; but when respite came, he was hardened. In misfortune, he was humbled and in health he was hardened. As if someone might say, 'I

> have raised up the head of this one who was sick and healed him; he was naked and I dressed him; he was poor and I made him rich; and look, today he opposes me.' In this way the Lord hardened Pharaoh through the good things he did to him and was compassionate upon him and by this gave him an opportunity for repentance. Because of this it was written, 'The Lord hardened the heart of Pharaoh—so that he would not obey.' That is, by means of compassion and [good] health Pharaoh was hardened.
>
> *pp. 278-9; cols. 705: 16 – 708: 12*

Reconciling a faith based upon the words of Scripture with the necessity for human free will exerts a great demand upon any spirituality. The author utilizes one of the more perplexing conundrums of the Biblical drama to reaffirm God's integrity—the so-called hardening of Pharaoh's heart by God. In a phrase, God killed Pharaoh with kindness. God had the fairness and compassion actually to listen and respond to Pharaoh's 'prayer' for help. Pharaoh would be humble when humbled, but arrogant and defiant when he felt powerful and at an advantage. No predestination is happening here, for in a back-handed way God's compassion—softness or gentleness—is what hardened Pharaoh's heart. Pharaoh, however, is really not an extraordinary exemplar of evil, so it is sobering to realize that he responds not much differently than the way we do in good and bad times. It is always easier to do and be good when things are going well for us and to be humble when we are humbled.

Mēmrā Twenty-Four
On repentance

Repentance and redemption are required for anyone who ranks below the step of Uprightness. God's mercifulness, which defies reason, created Uprightness as a way to escape the taste of death. The Perfect ones, on the other hand, have matured beyond the need for repentance and mercy, because they have no enemies in their hearts upon whom to be merciful.

> See how the Holy Spirit has spoken, 'If the Lord retains the former sins, no one is able to stand up before him, because everyone sins, but by repentance all will be received. Is there anyone who has defeated sin from the womb of his mother?' But human beings sin and repent and then they defeat sin, [that is,] those who continually battle strenuously and valiantly with [sin] everyday. A penitent person should not be compared to a coat or a wall, but we should compare them with something entering the fire. For, people are baptized in the Spirit, which is love and truth. Then, if they are prone to sin after they have been baptized, each time that they repent love is found for them to be baptized and purified. Just as when vessels of gold or of silver, brass, glass or iron, are broken, the worldly craftsman puts them into the physical fire, making them new and mending their features, and they are called 'new ones' after they had been worn out—how much more will God [do], the master craftsman, so that he might make them new in the fire that is love, and his spirit that is truth, and his waters [that] are faith?
>
> *pp. 284-5; cols. 717: 4 – 720: 2*

While the author aspires for Perfection for his charges, he recognizes that when someone does sin the world does not end for the sinner. After all, if judgment were to be exacted upon us on the basis of the number and nature of our sins, then no human being would remain standing. God, therefore, permits and encourages repentance by which one is purified as if by fire to become again 'a new being'. However, God's movement towards us does not work unless we are able to replicate God's forgiveness and renovation by our compassionate acceptance of neighbours who in reality sin no more grievously than us. We understand God by imitating God.

Mēmrā Twenty-Five
On the voice of God and Satan

A sermon calling upon both the Upright and the Perfect to distinguish correctly between the divine or satanic motives embedded in their manner of life. The author cautions the Perfect against being seduced into adopting the worldly ways of the Upright. The Upright are exhorted, on the other hand, not to cease their upward journey to Perfection.

> Look, [God] commanded the heavenly ones that they treat every person well with heavenly things. Where did you get the idea that no one should speak with a worthless or deceptive [person], because it may be [the case] that he will become a Perfect or an Upright one? As our Lord said to Ananias, 'Go, speak with Paul.' And Ananias said to our Lord, 'My Lord, he is an evil man, and I have heard of the affliction he has laid upon the saints who are in Jerusalem.' Our

> Lord replied to him, 'Go speak with him, because he is my chosen instrument, for you do not understand.' Therefore, in this way, [if] you have a word with anyone, speak, and you will not [thereby] sin.
>
> *p. 296; col. 745: 13-25*

Apparently, some of the Upright and Perfect ones were concerned to protect themselves and their purity from less desirable elements in society. The author reacts strongly to this move which he perceives to be motivated not by purity, but by pride and arrogance. One begins always with humility, considering every person better than oneself. Citing the familiar case of Ananias hosting the born-again Saul, the author cautions all to treat every person as if he or she were a Perfect one in the making, perhaps another Paul. Fools for Christ and authentic saints abound anonymously, although seldom is our best judgment able to identify them for who they really are. Purity derives from humility, not by physical separation from the non-Christian and the unworthy.

Mēmrā Twenty-Six
On the second law that the Lord established for Adam

A discourse directed to the Upright who live by the second law which God gave to Adam after his transgression of the first law. The Gospel of Jesus is the same one against which Adam transgressed, so with it still available there is hope for the Upright to reach Perfection.

> Therefore, after the first commandment, Adam and all the former Upright ones abided by that Uprightness that

God had commanded Adam after he had transgressed against the first word and became an earthly being. But if the remainder of the people had continued in this Uprightness that is written, in which Adam and the Upright ones journeyed, another law would not have been given to them until the Lord came and gave this Gospel for now. For the apostle said, 'The law was added to on account of error, this [law], which was given through Moses.'

p. 303; cols. 761: 19 – 764: 7

Now this Gospel, which Jesus gave, is the same one which Adam transgressed and [from which he] fell. That Uprightness that Moses and the prophets gave is the same one that was established for Adam after he had transgressed against the first commandment. So the first law became the latter law and the latter [law became] the first one, just as the last became the first and the first [became] the last. Whoever seeks Perfection and loves holiness, out of these things will come the holiness of the heart; he will give everything he has to the needy and ascend above whatever is visible. There will be controversy against him, yet he will neither judge nor demand [anything from] anyone, but will love everyone as a saint of our Lord, for he makes his love shine on everyone like the sun that the Father [causes to shine] upon all there is on the earth, whether good or evil, whether the just or the unjust.

p. 304; cols. 764: 23 – 765: 13

Once again, the goal of Jesus is not to usher us into the kingdom of heaven, but to lead us back to the Garden of Eden. The author's understanding of the dynamics of the divine economy perceives that the way of life and promises of the Gospel are the original covenant which God made with humanity in Eden. The sin in Eden—wanting to become like God—resulted in the creation of an alternative interim covenant with Adam and Eve and all their human descendants. This covenant, inscribed in stone on Sinai, is Uprightness. Only now Jesus proclaims not a new covenant, but a revived and renewed one.

Heaven or Eden may seem arbitrary, but rather than the Perfect ones working to transcend this world in order to acquire a new life, the classic Syriac scenario has the Perfect ones recovering their original life and image of God on earth. The author cautions, however, that re-entering Eden is not without controversy and conflict, for not everyone in human society finds the Perfect perfect.

Mēmrā Twenty-Seven
About the history of the thief who is saved

The title bears no apparent relation to the subject matter of the text, one of those accidents of ancient textual transmission. It is a sermonic discourse on one's readiness to suffer like Jesus on the way to Perfection. Concern is expressed for the spiritually immature lest they stray into idolatry or paganism. They should not leave home until they are mature enough to withstand the lies, slanders and injustices which they will surely incur on the Christian pilgrimage.

> Notice that on account of our stubbornness our parents complain, not on account of our lowliness. When your parents are very stubborn and evil, show them your lowliness [for] a year or a month or even ten days, and then depart. Do you think that when you depart, not being humble, you have defeated evil? That is when your struggles will multiply, when you depart from the company of your family. And if you do not have lowliness sin will corrupt you. But if you decide in your mind to endure everything that happens to you—falsehood, slander and injustice—while they are saying to you that you have committed adultery and fathered a child, and you are silent like a good rock, which is battered by a hundred pickaxes [and] does not say [anything, well and good]. Otherwise, do not depart, because you are still too young.
>
> *p. 307; cols. 772: 24 – 773: 23*

Continuing on the theme of the difficulties and persecution incurred by pursuers of Perfection and Uprightness, the author scolds some of his students to exhibit lowliness and humility before their critics, not stubborn pride in their spiritual accomplishments. The struggle to be an authentic Christian encounters much opposition, slander, and false accusations, even violence and death, so the mature Christian must not be discouraged or intimidated. Christians were far from the majority in fourth-century Persia, as perhaps is the case today even in Western societies. One's most reliable instrument is one's humility.

Mēmrā Twenty-Eight
On the fact that the human soul is not identical with the blood

A theological exposition on the inbreathing of the Holy Spirit, the Paraclete, given to the Perfect; and the lesser gift of the Holy Spirit to the Upright. The latter section of the *mēmrā* returns to the theme of the Visible Church as the image of the heavenly church: Abraham is an example of one who was saved while being married and having many possessions in this world.

> Consider Abraham and Sarah. After they had ceased carnal intercourse and their bodies were dead to desire, they obeyed the word of God and returned to having intercourse. In the same way, if God had told Abraham when he was young that he should keep himself holy from his wife, he would have kept himself holy, or if God had told him to empty himself, he would have emptied himself. Also, Abraham received the needy who did not even believe that God exists. He imitated God, who makes his love rise upon the good and the bad. For although everyone pities the good, one does not pity the bad, unless his love is great like our Lord's.
>
> *p. 320; cols. 804: 22 – 805: 7*

The closing paragraph of this *mēmrā* offers a different perspective on the spirituality of Abraham and Sarah. He is an apparently God-possessed person who lived a completely worldly existence, intercourse and income included. Yet the author believes that if God had called Abraham to a purely ascetical way of life, including celibacy and embracing poverty, he would not have hesitated. One way or the other, Abraham helped all those who were needy, not only the faithful poor but just as much those who denied God's existence. In this way, Abraham's love imitated God's. One does not have to be a celibate, possession-renouncing Perfect one to live out the Gospel. Abraham, the author believes, is an almost perfect example for the Upright ones and others attached still to the ways of this world.

Mēmrā Twenty-Nine
On the discipline of the body

A sermon directed to the entire church to conduct their ministry with passion and enthusiasm, not just 'by rote.' The author expresses concern over the lapses of the Perfect ones and exhorts the Upright ones to treat others well and follow their own rule.

> Look, my son, consider how much power is hidden in the praises of our Lord, yet we repeat them by rote without passion. Because of this, the words of God do not affect in us good deeds, for we do not give them a place in our soul to lay down roots in us. For that matter, even pagans, if they want, [can] learn the words of our Lord by rote at the same time they are worshipping in the house of their idols and doing the will of the devils.
>
> When one of us teaches his brother a psalm, saying to him, 'Refrain from rage and cease from anger', and [if] that teacher does not take it to heart, nor even does the disciple consider what his master is teaching him,

> look, are we not going through the motions without passion or knowledge? Because we do not do what we say, it is the same as if we do not know. Because of this the prophet said, 'I will think with my heart and speak with my mouth and make my voice heard'; that is, I will know what I am saying. 'Like a hart that longs for a pond of water, so also my soul longs for you, O Lord. My soul thirsts for you, living God, when may I come and see your face?' We are not as we teach, not knowing how to do [what we teach]. Even if a person reminds us that we ought to do thus we say, 'Yes', but look, are not the words of God playing in us, just like a dead cymbal in which there is no living soul, and we have learned by rote, and not with passion or with interior understanding?
>
> *p. 324; cols. 816: 17 – 817: 20*

The author has worked hard to construct a role for the Perfect and the Upright, but he knows all is in vain if all one does is follow the rules. Memorizing the prayers and appropriate responses is a mindless and soulless activity that non-Christians can do just as well as us. Humility and lowliness are the most important characteristics of a person pursuing Christian perfection, yet these too are a facade unless the Christian possesses passion, and passion is the requisite for a deeper understanding of the workings of the kingdom of heaven and the Garden of Eden. Nothing by rote, then; let us be consumed by every situation and every person as if for the first time.

Mēmrā Thirty
On the commandments of faith and the love of the solitaries

The second longest, and last, *mēmrā* begins by distinguishing between the commandments and disciples of faith and love—the latter being intermediate levels between the Upright and the Perfect. A summary of the standards of Perfection is rehearsed one last time. The author concludes the work with a strong affirmation of the ministry and salvation of the Upright ones, Zacchaeus being the model.

> Understand from this that people are saved if they do as they were commanded—[following] that precept that is lower than that perfect and superior precept, [even] while they are married and possessing wealth. [This is clear] by that demonstration when our Lord entered the house of Zacchaeus, a sinner and extortioner and doer of evil things, and admonishing him made him a disciple with these commandments that are inferior to Perfection.
>
> [Jesus] did not say to him, 'Unless you leave your wife and your house and your children and empty yourself from everything you own, you will not be saved.' Look, the response of Zacchaeus makes it clear that our Lord admonished him in such a way that he need not empty himself, because he knew that he could not reach the power of that great portion. Zacchaeus said, 'Everyone whom I have cheated I will repay four-fold, and half of my wealth only I will give to the poor. ' See, while he did not say to our Lord, 'I will abandon everything I have', our Lord did say the

> following to him, 'Today salvation has come into this house'. Zacchaeus shall be called a son of Abraham, he who when he promised to repay their lords what he had extorted had said, 'Half of my wealth only I will give'. But whoever gives to the poor half of his wealth while not defrauding anyone, look, is he not greater than Zacchaeus, who was called righteous? When he gave two portions of his wealth, look, does not he grow greater still? Whoever gives all he possesses to the poor and the strangers, look, is [that person] not better and greater?
>
> *p. 361; cols. 924: 13 – 925: 16*

The author is quite serious in this exegesis of the encounter between Jesus and Zacchaeus, but one cannot help be somewhat amused at the extent to which he stretches the text to affirm the validity of the Upright way of life. To be fair, the word 'only' does not occur in this particular text in the Syriac Peshitta New Testament. The author obviously heard this emphatic 'only' whispering between the lines. He remains emphatic in this last *mēmrā* that the goal of the Christian pilgrimage is not restricted to the Perfect who renounce completely this world in which we all have to travel. Zacchaeus actually did something to warrant his salvation, though considering his sordid past he did not overextend himself. Jesus' gracious acceptance of the master of extortion is really Good News, the Gospel; for as the author chides his readers, we can certainly do better than Zacchaeus.

One More Step

Reading what someone has written in the early centuries of Christianity is never a straightforward task. It is a naive expectation that the author will speak in clear twenty-first century English, for no translator can ever capture the tones of voice from long-dried ink on an ancient page. In the first place, not many people were writing texts in the fourth century and only a few more possessed the literacy to read them. The author of the *Book of Steps* wrote in Syriac, a Semitic language which, operating by a different grammatical system, 'thinks' differently than you and I do in English. We are always on a slightly different wavelength from our author, and in any case, he remained anonymous intentionally, which gives us even fewer clues about how his personality translates itself onto a page.

Yet, one of the paradoxes in religious thought and language is that, despite the above, you and I in the twenty-first century can understand what a fourth-century Semitic Christian is saying about the deep matters of the soul. Honouring the author's spirit as we read his words, our humility and lowliness enable us to listen at a different level. The realization that we cannot understand every detail should work to render us humble enough. So, let us rejoice in what we do understand and keep our inner ears open to learn a little bit more. By God's grace, may the Spirit inhabit us and may the Word indeed become flesh in us. In the midst of the Persian Empire, surrounded by a collection of Upright and Perfect Christians who never seem to get it right at the right time, this author without a name always was engaged in the quest of faith seeking understanding. He climbs the same steps as you and I.

Further Reading

The *Book of Steps: the Syriac* Liber Graduum, translation and introduction by Robert A. Kitchen & Martien F. G. Parmentier, Cistercian Studies 196; Kalamazoo, Michigan: Cistercian Publications, 2004.

Sebastian P. Brock, *The Syriac Fathers on Prayer and the Spiritual Life,* Cistercian Studies 101; Kalamazoo, Michigan: Cistercian Publications, 1987, pp. 42-61.

Robert Murray, *Symbols of Church and Kingdom,* revised edition, Piscataway, New Jersey: Gorgias Press, 2004, pp. 34-36, 263-269.

John Corbett, 'They Do Not Take Wives or Build, or Work the Ground: Ascetic Life in the Early Syriac Christian Tradition', *Canadian Journal of Syriac Studies 3,* 2003, pp. 3-20.

Robert A. Kitchen, 'Conflict on the Stairway to Heaven: The Anonymity of Perfection in the Syriac *Liber Graduum',* *Orientalia Christiana Analecta* 256 (1998) pp. 211-220.

'Becoming Perfect: The Maturing of Asceticism in the Syriac *Book of Steps', Canadian Journal of Syriac Studies 2,* 2002, pp. 30-45.

Kristian S. Heal and Robert A. Kitchen, *Breaking the Mind: New Studies in the Syriac* Book of Steps, Catholic University of America Studies in Early Christianity; Washington, DC: Catholic University of America Press, 2009.